My 12 Year Old Self and How I See the World

J Caldwell

Copyright © 2012 J Caldwell

All rights reserved.

ISBN: 978-0692052150

DEDICATION

I want to dedicate this book to all the youth in the world. Love yourself, be yourself and respect yourself!!

CONTENTS

    Acknowledgments

1. Hurt – Bullied — Page 1
2. Black Rights — Page 6
3. Poverty — Page 11
4. Beauty — Page 16
5. Being True to Yourself — Page 19
6. Haters — Page 23
7. Full Circle — Page 26
8. Family — Page 30
9. Love — Page 33
10. Friendship — Page 36
11. Goals — Page 41
12. Obstacles — Page 48
13. Education — Page 51
14. Growth — Page 55
15. Future — Page 68

ACKNOWLEDGMENTS

I want to thank my mother for acknowledging the messages I bring to poetry. My mother presented the idea of me writing a book of poetry and I was reluctant to do so. I wrote part of my book in South Carolina, but most of it in San Juan, Puerto Rico. This was the best summer ever! I was able to relax and write whenever the thoughts hit me, day or night!

My dad pushes me harder than anyone else and it drives me crazy! But, if my dad didn't push me as hard as he does to release the excellence that lives inside of me, I would settle for nothing. My parents are strong and bold as I am learning to be. I am learning to reach higher than I ever thought I could!

I would like to thank Ms. Karen, owner of Glam Dolls. She has showed me how to be confident, independent and simply be yourself!

Introduction

Hi, my name is Jordin and I am 12 years old. I am in middle school. I thought this would be the best time of my life. How very wrong I was. I been through some challenges, ups and downs, laughter, tears and plain old fun. But it was the hard times that got me thinking. I began to write my thoughts down, have discussions with my family, especially with my older cousins. They gave me tremendous insight into a lot of things I was naive about or just didn't understand. I believe "Life" is like a roller coaster.

Think about it, you go through mixed emotions on a roller coaster. I know I do. You start with fear, especially if it's a big roller coaster, fun, laughter, tears and most of all determination. You are determined you are going to ride this thing no matter what. You know if your friends are there, you are more pumped. So, I began writing my thoughts in poetic form of the many things that are going on in the world today and in my life.

This book will give you thought provoking messages, humor and maybe even tears. Remember people come and go, especially those who you thought were your friends.

Friends come a dime a dozen. In other words, you will only have a few that will become your closest friends. In middle school, you meet mean people, nice and comical people. Then there are the unique people who are themselves all the time, have their own style and march to their own beat. Well, that would be me "Miss Unique." I was criticized for being unique and often times called dumb, until those same people saw me receive my honors certificates while they sat watching. That was rewarding, but sad.

Judging people is all we do in middle school and it spills into our adulthood. I am here to give you a different point of view. Look at the big picture and open your minds. I know you hear our parents say, "The world is your oyster." Well, it's, because good oysters have pearls in them which makes them valuable and oh yeah, oysters are yummy to eat!! I'm just saying!

I hope you enjoy this book as well as I enjoyed writing it.

After each poem, there is a message I chose to provide to invoke thoughtful conversations. After you read each poem and message, there is a self-reflection page.

Smooches ☺ guys, I must go now. Enjoy!!!!!

Thought Provoking Poems
Messages
Self-Reflection Page

"POWER"

1 HURT - BULLIED

She was up every morning knowing her day will be miserable

She goes to school every day drained from crying

She put on a fake smile

She always asks a person to walk with her in the hallways, knowing no one likes her

She sit in front with her desk facing the wall in her math class

She cringes as she hears the girls talk about her

She gets quiet and they begin to throw things at her

The girls are like sharks that smell blood

They attack one lone person as if they are walking on the beach and are now their prey

They tear you apart!

Yeah, that's how she felt every day

The girls have rallied others to post mean things on "Social Media"

They post things like "Hoe" "Thot" Slut" just to ruin her reputation because she easily made friends with boys

She lost some friends but learned that everyone is not your friend

The girls stop at nothing and send rude and hurtful things!

You see, these girls were once her friends

Since she told these girls no she can't or no she couldn't, they decided she could no longer be their friend!

The bullying continued non-stop!

She got even sadder and thought about taking her life.

She talked about it with her very close friend and close family.

She was broken down even more by a text she received from a girl she never had a problem with resulting in threats of bodily harm.

She broke down, cried and didn't go to school that day and never returned to that school ever again!

She had no trust or faith in the school, teachers or the principal – there was no safe zone!

She felt alone and nowhere to go

She is me and I am no more the victim of bullying, I am an advocate against bullying!!!

My Thoughts

Self-Reflection Lesson #1 Bullying

Have you ever been bullied or are you the bully? Is it worth it to degrade someone's self-worth for a moment of satisfaction and laughter? How would you feel if you were being bullied? Why is all I ask? Reach across and get to know someone that you normally would not speak to. You will be surprised at the things you may learn or what you may have in common. TRY IT!!

Your Thoughts
Self-Reflection

NO MORE BULLYING!!

NO MORE VIOLENCE!!

2 BLACK RIGHTS

Blacks are getting killed by cops for standing up and believing in their RIGHTS!

Since slavery, getting beaten because they try to escape or try to learn how to read and write;

Had bombs thrown at their homes, destroyed everything and sometimes took the lives of loved ones.

Blacks had to fight for their RIGHTS since the beginning of time!

Blacks got shot for having a dream that blacks and whites can get along, or get lynched for whistling at a white woman.

Look at some of our *Greats* that have been assassinated like Dr. Martin Luther King Jr., Medgar Evers and Malcolm X for standing up and speaking about BLACK RIGHTS!

Blacks get shot for having their hands up and BOOM! Goes the sound of the gun.

My 12 Year Old Self and How I See the World

Gunsmoke fills the air – dead silence – screams – witnesses – sirens all because of the sound of the gun & a lifeless body on the ground.

Some of the fallen victims are Trayvon Martin, Sandra Bland, Tamar Rice & Eric Garner!

The hurt and tears are like dark nights with heavy showers.

The deaths of the victims bring turmoil, uprising, and protest in our communities!

Some protests are quiet and orderly.

Some protests are loud and violent!

The media focus on the negativity, drawn from protests instead of the message.

The media are like bees drawn to honey gone bad. They don't care that it tastes bitter, they want more and release it for the communities to grasp hold on.

Some cling to the bitter honey and some release it to find a better honeycomb that leads them out of the dark hole and into the light of truth!

Blacks are recognized for stealing and violence, but can't be recognized for the good things they do!

There are many blacks that are positive role models, powerful, successful and beautiful spirited people that outweigh the bad!

FACE IT – We all have good & bad people in every race!

Blacks are many times portrayed in a negative manner on T.V. and in movies when we have so much more to offer!

Why don't Blacks have bigger roles on T.V. or in the movies?

Blacks don't get paid fairly compared to their white counterparts. Again I ask why?

I think blacks need bigger roles, get paid fairly and recognized for what they have contributed to society!

As a black girl, I have been followed in stores with my friends and even with my parents;

Why? Is it necessary to follow us? Do you think we don't have any money or do you think we are going to steal? What is it?

OUR VOICE MATTERS! Everyone's voice matters!

If being treated fairly was the norm there would be equality.

It is 2017 and we are still facing the issue of blacks getting shot or killed.

Blacks have to stand up for their RIGHTS and never GIVE UP!

My Thoughts

Self-Reflection Lesson #2 Discrimination

Does color, gender or sexuality matter? I know some of you are thinking, why did I use the word sexuality? Well, it is in our faces every day. Does it matter if you are "gay or straight"? Does it matter what color you are? Does it matter how much money your family has? Does it matter if you are a boy or girl? Why are we judged because of our race? IS THAT FAIR I ASK? NO, IT ISN'T!!!

I challenge you to look in the mirror and ask these questions. Better yet, do a survey with family and friends. Keep an open mind.

Remember being judged isn't comfortable or fun!!!

Your Thoughts
Self-Reflection

3 POVERTY

People are slowly dying because of world hunger, no shelter, no money, no food, no clothes or no job.

They sit on the streets and ask for money day in and day out.

This isn't how their life should be.

Kids and adults are homeless, and all I ask is why?

Our veterans who fought for our country are homeless.

People use their money for the finest things but can't help those who need it most.

Let's end world hunger and poverty in all of the United States and all over the world!

Giving back is also called sharing and sharing is what we should teach!

I give back and I challenge you to do it too;

Giving back is a feeling like no other!

My Thoughts

Self-Reflection Lesson #3 Poverty

Poverty is the struggle that many people face. Many kids go without food and wear worn or 2nd hand clothes. Some are sad and some are surrounded by so much love. Some follow the streets, which often lead to drugs, gangs, violence, death or jail. Being poor or underprivileged does not define you or your future!! Don't fall into the trap of what society believes will ultimately happen to poor or the underprivileged. Take advantage of all the opportunities that are available to us. Talk to people! You never know what you may learn, who you may meet or what the blessing may come through conversation with others.

Your Thoughts
Self-Reflection

LOVE YOURSELF

My 12 Year Old Self and How I See the World

SIMPLY BEAUTIFUL

4 BEAUTY

Beauty comes in different shapes, sizes, color, age, and style.

*The true meaning of **Beauty** is you!*

You shine brightly when you walk into a room.

Don't let anyone dim your light.

God is the reason why you are so beautiful today and every day!

Smile, embrace and love yourself.

My Thoughts

Self-Reflection Lesson #4 Beauty

Beauty is in the eye of the beholder. You are beautiful inside and out. Always remember a beautiful personality and beautiful spirit goes a long way. Take care of yourself and your health. Believe in yourself and treat everyone with kindness and respect!

Be yourself
Embrace yourself
Accept yourself
Uniquely you are
Truthfulness
You are beautiful

J Caldwell

Your Thoughts
Self-Reflection

5 BEING TRUE TO YOURSELF

I have a mind of my own

I don't care what people say

I will not change for others

I am able to change when I see flaws in myself

I love myself

I am **#1**

My Thoughts

Self-Reflection Lesson #5 Being True To Yourself

Wake up and be thankful for another day. Look in the mirror and tell yourself you are worthy and you love yourself. Believe in yourself! Never let anyone try to change you or destroy you. Remember to take care of your heart, mind, and soul.

Your Thoughts
Self-Reflection

"I'M HERE – I'M STILLL STANDING"

6 HATERS

Haters they cater you with all the beef they have on you.

Haters, they're like players who play games with you like **2K17**.

Haters they hate on you because you are **POPPIN!**

You stunt on them, so they hate you more!!

Dust your shoulder off and fix your crown,

Let them **Haters** hate on you and you be the Queen or King that you are!!

My Thoughts

Self-Reflection Lesson #6 Haters = Jealousy

Jealousy gets you nowhere, but headaches and frustration. Why should you be jealous of someone because of material things or if they are a genuinely likable person? Look in the mirror and tell yourself you are worth so much more. All the material things in the world and the number of friends I have does not define who I am.

Your Thoughts

7 FULL CIRCLE

Maturing

Accepting me for me

Believing in myself with some self-doubt

Building up my self-confidence and self-esteem

Knowing my self-worth

Empowers me and others around me!

My Thoughts

Self-Reflection Lesson #7 Full Circle

Full circle is learning who you are and who you want to become. Through all of life's lessons, mistakes, encounters, bumps and falls you will become the person who has been shaped by everything you have gone through. I am in the beginning stages of full circle and as an adult, will one day look back and say, "It was all worth it!"

Your Thoughts
Self-Reflection

My 12 Year Old Self and How I See the World

NEW BEGINNINGS

8 FAMILY

Family never ends;

A family is like a tree, it keeps growing.

Family and friends sometimes become one;

There is family that you meet for the first time,

Bonding with them strengthens the family.

Family brings love, joy, heartache, and laughter!

Through it all, we are family.

A loving family always sticks together through thick and thin.

Remember to love your family as they will always love you!

My 12 Year Old Self and How I See the World

My Thoughts

Self-Reflection Lesson #8 Family

Some families are huge and some are small. Some of us have siblings and some of us don't, like me. There are times I am lonely and often have to entertain myself. Sometimes that is great and sometimes not. I find myself developing sibling relationships with my cousins or new friends. I also spend lots of time with my parents. We tell jokes, laugh, talk and spend quality time together.

I have learned, no matter how mad I may get at my family, the ones who truly love me are always there. That's what I call a loving family!

Your Thoughts
Self-Reflection

9 LOVE

Love is very powerful!

It is a feeling of happiness ☺

Have you ever felt love, embraced love, seen love or received love?

Love is a feeling that never goes away, but when it dies it's gone!

Love comes in all forms;

Love comes from your family and friends.

Sadly, there are those who have never been loved or experienced love, not even from their own family ☹

Don't let love go to waste, it's too valuable!

Don't give up on love☺

I will always love myself 1st because I am worthy of LOVE!

My Thoughts

Self-Reflection Lesson #9 Love

As a child how do you describe love? I am not talking about the schoolboy or schoolgirl crush we develop as an adolescent. Is love showing or giving affection? Is love lending a listening ear? Is love having parents who shower you with gifts? I believe love is a feeling deep within. You feel loved whenever you are around the people who love you most and who you love.

J Caldwell

Your Thoughts
Self-Reflection

10 FRIENDSHIP

Friendship is like a bond that can't be broken.

When you first meet that person, there is an automatic connection.

You seem to have everything in common,

You believe your friendship will never end.

Arguments and fights may occur and you still remain best friends.

When you find a real and true friend, cherish that bond.

Everyone that pretends to be your friend is not your friend!

#Bondcan'tbebroken

My Thoughts

Self-Reflection Lesson #10 Friendship

Friend is a tricky word. My mom once told me that Daisy's grow in bunches and they are looked upon as my associates. Roses' need nurturing and take a while to grow along a vine. My mom said I am a rose and my true friends will grow with me along a vine.

Think of friendship as a recipe. You pour bits of your personality into a mixing bowl. The person you meet pours bits of their personality into the same mixing bowl. Together you have blended a mix of ingredients poured in from your personalities. This mix has become a unique blended recipe called friendship. Each friendship is uniquely blended and can never be duplicated, except for the steps in building a new friendship!

Time, patience and nurturing are foundations for a true friendship. I am learning who I am as I am learning what a friend really is. Always remember you have control over who you let into your circle. You have the ability to open and close your circle at any given time. So be careful who you let into your circle, which includes your space and your energy. Any of the wrong elements can change you and your life forever!

LET THE FUN TIMES BEGIN!

Your Thoughts
Self-Reflection

HARD WORK PAYS OFF!

11 GOALS

Goals look straight ahead in your life;

The reach seems almost impossible.

Goals keep the past in the past and your future in the present.

Your future is the most important thing in your life.

Set your goals – plan for it – strive for it and reach for it!

Work hard for it and you will be successful in accomplishing your goals.

DREAM BIG AND IN COLOR!!!

My Thoughts

Self-Reflection Lesson #11 Goals

Goals are meant to be set. You must first define your goals and plan how to achieve your goals. It is ok to make adjustments along the way. Don't let anything or anyone stop you from reaching your goals.

Remember if you say I am trying, you are already setting yourself up for failure. Nothing beats a failure but a try. I know this may make you go um ☹??? I thought the same thing.

Simply think of this: If you never try for something, you will never know if you can achieve it. If you say you are trying, then you are not giving it your all. Now that's better right?

.

#GOALS

#HARDWORK

#DEDICATION

#DON'T STOP

Your Thoughts
Self-Reflection

LIVE, LOVE LAUGH & LEARN ☺

NO OBSTACLES ALLOWED

Don't Stop **Me Now!** I'm on the Move!

12 OBSTACLES

Obstacles are like people who want to see you fail.

You got to push through them or jump over them like hurdles.

Obstacles are roadblocks that you have to go around or make a detour.

Never let any obstacle stop you from getting to the finish line!

You may make some mistakes and have some setbacks, but don't let it stop you.

Don't let yourself or others stand in your way,

Stay determined, focused and passionate about your dreams.

Strive to achieve anything you set your mind to.

You are a winner!!

My Thoughts

Self-Reflection Lesson #12 Obstacles

Obstacles are like road blocks. Sometimes the roadblocks are people, things or even yourself. Yep, you are thinking how can I be my own road block?

Well if you let fear take over, then you have set up a roadblock.

If you are always 2nd guessing yourself, that's another roadblock.

Don't block your blessing. Keep the negativity away from you. These roadblocks can ultimately determine your future.

Then there are obstacles that are meant to teach you lessons and make you stronger. These obstacles are the ones that have been set for you as a test in life. God is always working for us and preparing us to be ready to open and receive the message. These messages and people are like waves. You will begin to learn this from childhood to adulthood.

Your Thoughts
Self-Reflection

13 EDUCATION

Education is very important.

Education is a tool that you use in school and in your life.

Learning is so critical!

Knowledge is the key to unlock the doors of the universe;

For me and my mind, it is important;

It is unparalleled even through my distractions and self-doubt.

Without education, you limit yourself to the possibilities of what can and what could be.

Reading, writing, listening and learning are the basics of getting an education.

I can do it and I know you can too!

Don't throw your education away and don't take it for granted!

My Thoughts
Self-Reflection

Self-Reflection Lesson #13 Education

Respect yourself, respect your school and respect your teachers. These are the 3 main keys to our success. You must be willing to learn, explore, listen, study, read, and have healthy conversations. Give it all you got, to fully understand and receive an education.

Going to school with a great environment makes students want to learn and feel safe. Having teachers that are willing to teach beyond the regular scope of learning is a bonus. Remember you, your teacher and your school count! Not only the building but the staff that runs the school. Our parents, family, neighbors, etc. are the reinforcement to help when you need help. "Don't be Afraid to Ask Questions!" "Don't be Afraid to Help Others!"

REMEMBER: Create those fun moments while you are still a kid. I see my parents and their friends reminisce about when they were in school. The laugh and share stories. I want those memories, laughter and still get a good education!

Your Thoughts
Self-Reflection

I AM WORTHY – I AM THE FUTURE

14 GROWTH

Growth is the most important thing in everyone's life.

Your life is the seed

It grows like a tree that stretches with many branches.

The branches represent life and the leaves represent people.

Every time you age or learn something new, you grow!

When growth happens, your seed keeps developing.

Growth grows into a full tree, which represents maturity and strength!

Growth is a good thing!

My Thoughts

Self-Reflection Lesson #14 Growth

Growth is about maturity and learning from life's lessons. Your mind will grow the more you learn. Having a growth mindset is all about having an open mind. Your body will physically grow. You will notice and see a change in your appearance as you will notice the change in your attitude and actions. Growth is a beautiful thing!

Your Thoughts
Self-Reflection

15 FUTURE

Freedom to be who you want to be

Understanding who you are and know that you control your future

Teaching, talking and time are elements of you that will direct you

Unfinished work is call procrastination

Reading is fundamental to your future

Educate yourself, because Knowledge is Power!!!

My Thoughts

Self-Reflection Lesson #15 Future

My future is what I make it. What will your future be? Take this time to think about your future and work towards the future you wish to have. I know I will!!!

ABOUT THE AUTHOR

J Caldwell has many talents and enjoys expressing herself creatively. J wants to be a pastry chef and open her own bakery one day. She loves cake art and creatively decorating cupcakes and cakes. She was the only child in her cake decorating class with a group of adults and she was not intimidated. This speaks volumes about her passion and dedication. She has her own cupcake business that she started at the age of 10. She is a self-taught gymnast, dancer and dabbled a bit in karate. She is a natural. Fashion, modeling, and acting are some of her favorite things to do too. Going to a good play, a movie, studying the characters, a script or the making of a movie gives her great passion. A few of her all-time favorite things to do is watching a documentary, a bio movie or going to museums. J has done this since she was four years old! Writing poetry was another form of art J wanted to try. Her words and expressions reveal how well rounded she is. J does not let a lot of her friends or teachers see this side of her. Her gifts are sometimes hidden by choice. J's parents encourage her to be her true self and let the world see how gifted she is. J describes poetry as having no boundaries and lets her be as creative as she wants to be, in a few words or a few pages. J loves the freedom of creativity!